First Facts®

GODS and GODDESSES
of ❧Ancient Greece❧

by Danielle Smith-Llera

Consultant:
Jonathan M. Hall
Phyllis Fay Horton Distinguished Service Professor
in the Humanities
The University of Chicago

CAPSTONE PRESS
a capstone imprint

First Facts are published by Capstone Press,
1710 Roe Crest Drive, North Mankato, Minnesota 56003
www.capstonepub.com

Library of Congress Cataloging-in-Publication Data

Smith-Llera, Danielle, 1971–
Gods and goddesses of ancient Greece / Danielle Smith-Llera.
pages cm.—(Ancient Greece)
Includes bibliographical references and index.
ISBN 978-1-4914-0274-0 (library binding)
ISBN 978-1-4914-0279-5 (eBook PDF)
Summary: "Describes Greek gods and goddesses and some stories about them from ancient Greek Mythology"—Provided by publisher.
1. Gods, Greek. 2. Goddesses, Greek. 3. Mythology, Greek. 4. Greece—Religion. I. Title.
BL783.S655 2015
292.2'11—dc23   2013049476

Editorial Credits

Aaron Sautter, editor; Bobbie Nuytten, designer; Svetlana Zhurkin, media researcher; Jennifer Walker, production specialist

Printed in China by Nordica
0414/CA21400593
032014   008095NORDF14

TABLE OF CONTENTS

WATCHING FROM THE MOUNTAIN

The ancient Greeks honored and worshiped several gods and goddesses. They believed the gods watched over people from their home on Mount Olympus. The Greeks thought the gods controlled things such as earthquakes, the weather, and when people died. Today we know Greek gods were just **myths**. Let's look at the family of Greek gods and what people once believed about them.

myth—a story told by people in ancient times; myths often tried to explain natural events

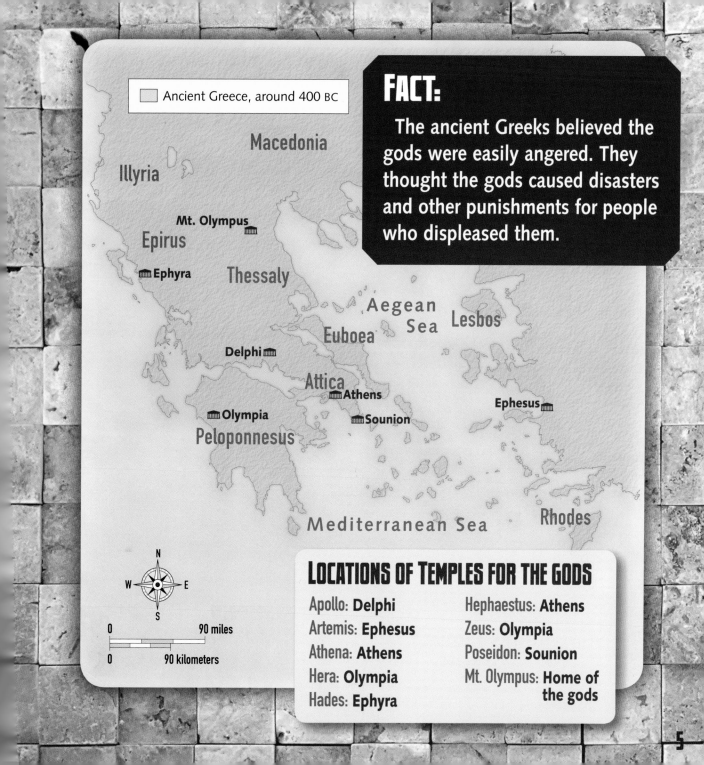

Ancient Greece, around 400 BC

Illyria

Macedonia

Epirus

Mt. Olympus

Ephyra

Thessaly

Aegean Sea

Lesbos

Euboea

Delphi

Attica

Athens

Ephesus

Olympia

Sounion

Peloponnesus

Mediterranean Sea

Rhodes

FACT:

The ancient Greeks believed the gods were easily angered. They thought the gods caused disasters and other punishments for people who displeased them.

N
W E
S

0   90 miles
0   90 kilometers

LOCATIONS OF TEMPLES FOR THE GODS

Apollo: **Delphi**

Artemis: **Ephesus**

Athena: **Athens**

Hera: **Olympia**

Hades: **Ephyra**

Hephaestus: **Athens**

Zeus: **Olympia**

Poseidon: **Sounion**

Mt. Olympus: **Home of the gods**

5

ZEUS

Zeus was king over the sky and all the Greek gods. The ancient Greeks believed Zeus controlled the weather. They also thought Zeus had a bad temper. When he was displeased, he hurled thunderbolts at those who angered him. However, stories also show that Zeus tried to rule fairly and shared power with his family.

FACT:

One story about Zeus tells about Typhon, a fierce monster with 100 serpent heads. When Typhon attacked Mount Olympus, all the other gods fled. But Zeus defeated him by picking up Mount Aetna and burying Typhon underneath it.

A huge statue of Zeus was once considered one of the wonders of the ancient world.

HERA

Hera was Zeus' wife and the goddess of marriage. But Zeus often fell in love with human women. Zeus had a son, Heracles, with a human woman. This made Hera **jealous** and angry. When Heracles was a baby, Hera sent snakes to try to kill him.

jealous—to want something someone else has

FACT:

Greek women prayed to Hera for help to find husbands and to have children.

ruins of a temple for Hera in Italy

POSEIDON

Zeus' brother Poseidon ruled the seas. Greeks trembled at his changing moods. With his **trident**, Poseidon could make the earth quake and the seas rise. The Greeks believed floods were Poseidon's punishment for those who displeased him. When the seas were calm, sailors believed Poseidon was content.

trident—a long spear with three sharp points at its end

HADES

Greeks feared meeting Hades—the god of the dead. Even Hades' brother Zeus avoided him. The Greeks believed that Hades punished people who disrespected the gods. Hades' three-headed dog, Cerberus, is found in several Greek myths. Cerberus guarded the entrance to the **Underworld** and kept the dead from escaping.

Underworld—the place under the earth where ancient Greeks believed spirits of the dead went

HADES AND SISYPHUS

In one story a king named Sisyphus used several tricks to escape death. But Hades finally captured him. As punishment for his tricks, Hades forced Sisyphus to push a boulder up a steep hill. But it always rolled back down. Sisyphus was forced to repeat his punishment forever.

ATHENA

Zeus' favorite child, Athena, was the goddess of wisdom. She often helped people. Athena gave Perseus a special shield, which he used to defeat the snake-haired monster, Medusa. But Athena could also be **spiteful**. In one myth a woman claimed to weave more beautifully than Athena. The goddess punished the woman by turning her into a spider.

spiteful—a desire to hurt, annoy, or offend someone

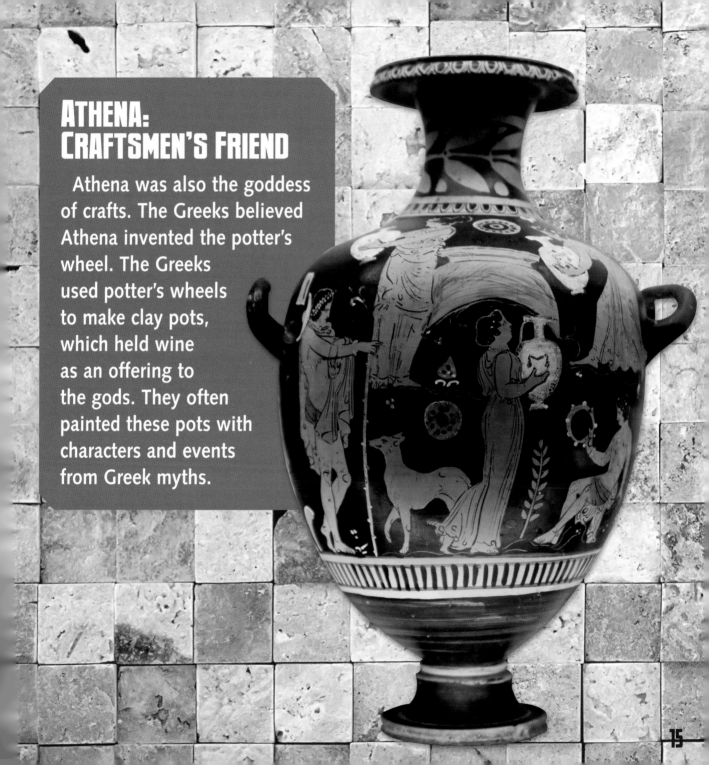

ATHENA: CRAFTSMEN'S FRIEND

Athena was also the goddess of crafts. The Greeks believed Athena invented the potter's wheel. The Greeks used potter's wheels to make clay pots, which held wine as an offering to the gods. They often painted these pots with characters and events from Greek myths.

ARTEMIS

Artemis was the goddess of hunting. She enjoyed life in the forest with her bow and silver arrows. This daughter of Zeus never married. She preferred hunting with female friends. The Greeks believed Artemis protected children. She also watched over young women until they married.

FACT:

One Greek myth says that a hunter once spied on Artemis as she bathed in a lake. Artemis became very angry and turned him into a deer. His own hunting dogs then killed him.

a sculpture of the hunter who was punished by Artemis in Caserta, Italy

APOLLO

Artemis' handsome twin brother, Apollo, was Zeus' favorite son. This proud god of music loved playing his stringed **lyre**. Apollo had a short temper. One story says he once gave donkey ears to a king who disliked his music. But Apollo was also generous. The Greeks believed that he allowed visitors to see their own futures at his temple in Delphi.

APOLLO IN LOVE

One myth tells about how Apollo fell in love with a **nymph** named Daphne. When he chased after her, she turned into a laurel tree to escape him. But Apollo still loved Daphne. So he took care of the laurel tree and claimed it as his symbol. The Greeks often used laurel leaves to crown leaders and winners of competitions.

lyre—a small, stringed, harplike instrument
nymph—a beautiful female spirit or goddess who lived on a mountain, in a forest, or in a body of water

HEPHAESTUS

Hephaestus walked with a limp and relied on a walking stick. The Greeks believed his mother, Hera, tossed him off Mount Olympus because he was so ugly. Inside a volcano Hephaestus learned to be a **blacksmith**. He created powerful weapons and armor such as Zeus' thunderbolts and Athena's shield. Hephaestus later returned to Mount Olympus as the god of metalwork and fire.

blacksmith—someone who makes and fixes metal objects

Family Tree of the Gods

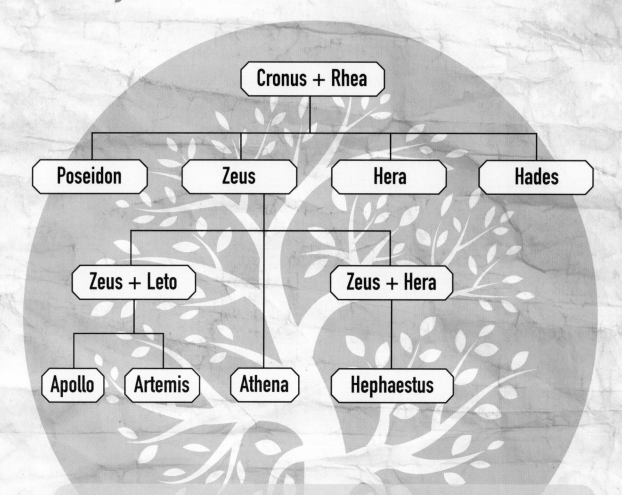

The Greek gods and goddesses were all part of one big family. Like human families, they were all related to one another as brothers, sisters, aunts, uncles, and cousins.

Glossary

blacksmith (BLAK-smith)—someone who makes and fixes metal objects

jealous (JEL-uhss)—to want something someone else has

lyre (LIRE)—a small, stringed, harplike instrument

myth (MITH)—a story told by people in ancient times; myths often tried to explain natural events

nymph (NIMF)—a beautiful female spirit or goddess who lived on a mountain, in a forest, or in a body of water

spiteful (SPYT-fuhl)—a desire to hurt, annoy, or offend someone

trident (TRY-dent)—a long spear with three sharp points at its end

Underworld (UHN-dur-wurld)—the place under the Earth where ancient Greeks believed spirits of the dead went

Read More

Hunt, Jilly. *Greek Myths and Legends*. All About Myths. Chicago: Raintree, 2013.

Meister, Cari. *The Battle of the Olympians and the Titans: A Retelling*. Greek Myths. Mankato, Minn.: Picture Window Books, 2012.

O'Connor, George. *Zeus: King of the Gods*. Olympians. New York: First Second, 2010.

Internet Sites

FactHound offers a safe, fun way to find Internet sites related to this book. All of the sites on FactHound have been researched by our staff.

Here's all you do:

Visit *www.facthound.com*

Type in this code: 9781491402740

Check out projects, games and lots more at
www.capstonekids.com

Critical Thinking Using the Common Core

1. In your own words, explain why the ancient Greeks believed that the gods controlled everything that happened in the world. (Integration of Knowledge and Ideas)

2. Look at the Family Tree of the Gods on page 21. How were Zeus, Poseidon, and Hades related to each other? (Craft and Structure)

Index